How to Rizz Guide to Being Cool and Flirting

Table of Contents

Chapter 1: The Origin of Rizz: Getting Rizzed Up

What the Heck is Rizz?

Yo, welcome to the world of Rizz! If you're reading this, you're probably wondering what this whole "Rizz" thing is about. Sit tight, grab some snacks, and let me take you on a wild ride through the origins of Rizz.

Back in the day, people used to call it "game" or "swagger." But as the times changed, so did the lingo. And now, the coolest term on the block is "Rizz." Rizz is that special sauce you got when you're smooth, charming, and just plain irresistible. It's like charisma, but on steroids. When you've got Rizz, you can walk into a room and make everyone's heads turn—no cap.

Imagine you're at a party. The music's bumping, and everyone's mingling. Suddenly, someone walks in and immediately becomes the center of attention. They've got the looks, the moves, and the vibe that makes everyone want to be around them. That's Rizz. It's not just about being noticed; it's about being unforgettable.

Getting Rizzed Up

To get rizzed up means to level up your cool factor to legendary status. It's like when Mario eats a mushroom and goes from zero to hero, except you're not in a video game, and there's no mushroom (unless you're into fungi, then you do you).

When you get rizzed up, you're the life of the party, the star of the show, the person everyone wants to be around. You're spitting fire without even trying. You're basically the human version of a TikTok trend that never dies.

Picture this: you're in the cafeteria, and you see your crush sitting with their friends. You walk over, crack a joke that makes everyone laugh, and suddenly, all eyes are on you. That's Rizz in action. It's about having that magnetic energy that draws people in and makes them want more.

The Birth of Rizz

The term "Rizz" didn't just pop out of nowhere. It evolved from the streets, from the digital realms of TikTok, Instagram, and all those places where cool kids hang out. Rizz is a vibe, a state of mind, a way of life. It's about having the confidence to be yourself and the charm to make others fall head over heels for you.

In the age of social media, where everyone's trying to stand out, Rizz has become the ultimate currency. It's not just about how you look but how you carry yourself. It's about the way you talk, the way you walk, and the way you make people feel. And trust me, once you tap into your Rizz, there's no going back.

The Evolution of Rizz

Let's take a quick trip down memory lane. Back in the stone age (like, the 2000s), Rizz was just starting to take shape. The seeds were planted by the early internet—MySpace, anyone? People were figuring out how to stand out and be noticed. Fast forward to the age of Instagram and TikTok, and boom—Rizz exploded onto the scene.

Social media became the perfect breeding ground for Rizz. From viral challenges to influencer culture, the game was all about who had the most Rizz. And it wasn't just about looking good in selfies; it was about the entire package—personality, humor, confidence, and that special something that made people double-tap on your posts.

The Anatomy of Rizz

To understand Rizz, we need to break it down. Here are the key components that make up Rizz:

1. **Confidence**: This is the backbone of Rizz. Without confidence, you're just another face in the crowd.
2. **Charisma**: The ability to charm and captivate people. It's like being a human magnet.
3. **Humor**: Making people laugh is a surefire way to earn Rizz points.

4. **Authenticity**: Being genuine and true to yourself. No one likes a phony.
5. **Body Language**: How you carry yourself. This includes posture, eye contact, and gestures.
6. **Style**: Your personal look. This doesn't mean you have to be a fashion icon, but having a sense of style helps.

Case Study: The Legend of Chad and Stacy

Let's talk about Chad and Stacy, the ultimate Rizz power couple. Chad was the guy everyone wanted to be. He had confidence, could talk to anyone, and was always the life of the party. Stacy was the queen bee—beautiful, smart, and effortlessly cool. When they got together, their combined Rizz was off the charts.

But here's the kicker: neither Chad nor Stacy were born with Rizz. They worked at it. Chad used to be awkward and shy, and Stacy was super insecure. They both decided to work on themselves—Chad started practicing his conversation skills, and Stacy embraced her unique style. They didn't just magically become cool overnight; they put in the effort.

Chapter 2: Obtain Your Inner Rizz

Finding the Rizz Within

Alright, now that you know what Rizz is, it's time to find yours. Everyone's got Rizz inside them, just waiting to be unleashed. Think of it as your personal superpower. But instead of fighting crime, you're fighting for the attention of that cutie in math class.

Step 1: Confidence is Key

First things first, you gotta believe in yourself. Confidence is the cornerstone of Rizz. If you walk around like you're the main character in a movie, people are gonna notice. Hold your head high, make eye contact, and flash those pearly whites. If you believe you're awesome, others will too.

Scenario: You're at a school dance, and you see your crush standing by the punch bowl. Instead of overthinking it, you take a deep breath, walk over, and start a conversation. Your confidence catches their attention, and before you know it, you're dancing together.

Step 2: Be Yourself

No one likes a fake. Being genuine is a huge part of having Rizz. If you're trying to be someone you're not, people will see right through it. Embrace your quirks and own them. Whether you're into Dungeons & Dragons or K-pop, let your freak flag fly. Authenticity is attractive AF.

Scenario: You're in class, and the teacher asks everyone to share their hobbies. Instead of trying to fit in, you proudly talk about your love for comic books. Surprisingly, your crush is also into comics, and just like that, you've found common ground. Being yourself pays off.

Step 3: Master the Art of Conversation

Good Rizz means you can talk to anyone about anything. Practice makes perfect, so start chatting up strangers, friends, your dog—whoever will listen. Keep the convo light, funny, and engaging. Ask questions and actually listen to the answers. Remember, it's not all about you.

Scenario: You're at a friend's party, and you find yourself in a conversation with someone you've never met. Instead of feeling awkward, you ask them about their favorite movies. The conversation flows, and by the end of the night, you've made a new friend (and maybe even impressed your crush).

Step 4: The Power of Body Language

Your body language speaks volumes. Stand tall, don't slouch, and avoid crossing your arms. Use gestures to emphasize points and make sure your face is as expressive as your words. And for the love of all things holy, don't forget to smile. It's the universal sign of friendliness.

Scenario: You're at a family gathering, and your relatives introduce you to someone your age. Instead of standing awkwardly, you maintain good posture, make eye contact, and engage in the conversation with a smile. Your positive body language makes a great impression.

Developing Your Unique Style

Part of having Rizz is looking the part. Now, this doesn't mean you need to wear the latest designer clothes or follow every fashion trend. Your style should be a reflection of who you are. Here's how to develop a style that screams Rizz:

1. **Know Your Body Type**: Wear clothes that fit well and flatter your body type. Baggy clothes or outfits that are too tight can be a turn-off.
2. **Find Your Colors**: Discover which colors complement your skin tone and make you look vibrant.
3. **Accessories**: Don't underestimate the power of accessories. A cool watch, necklace, or even a funky pair of socks can add a lot to your outfit.

4. **Grooming**: Good grooming is essential. Make sure you're well-groomed—hair, nails, and even skincare. A fresh look goes a long way.

Scenario: You're going out with friends, and you decide to put a little extra effort into your outfit. You wear a well-fitted shirt, your favorite jeans, and a cool pair of sneakers. You add a stylish watch and make sure your hair is on point. As soon as you walk into the room, people notice your upgraded look.

Practicing Positivity

Positivity is infectious and a crucial part of Rizz. Nobody wants to be around a Debbie Downer. Here's how to cultivate a positive mindset:

1. **Practice Gratitude**: Take a moment each day to think about what you're grateful for. This shifts your focus from what you lack to what you have.
2. **Avoid Negative Talk**: Try not to engage in gossip or negative conversations. Keep things light and positive.
3. **Encourage Others**: Lift

Quality Over Quantity

When it comes to social media, less is more. Instead of flooding your feed with every photo you take, post the best ones—the ones that make you look like a snack. Quality content makes a bigger impact than quantity.

Scenario: You're out with friends, and you take a killer group photo. Instead of posting every picture from the night, you pick the best one where you look confident and happy. Your followers will notice the quality over the quantity.

Engage

Social media isn't just about broadcasting your life; it's about engaging with others. Comment on posts, reply to stories, and slide into DMs like a pro. Just don't be creepy. Keep it light and fun.

Scenario: Your crush posts a picture of their new puppy. You leave a funny comment like, "I think your puppy just stole my heart!" It's light, engaging, and gets you noticed.

Memes

Share funny memes. Everyone loves a good meme. It shows you have a sense of humor and keeps the vibe light.

Scenario: You find a hilarious meme about school and share it on your story. Your crush replies with a laughing emoji, and just like that, you've started a conversation.

The Art of Flirting

Flirting is an essential Rizz skill. Here's how to do it without coming off as a total weirdo.

Subtlety

Less is more. A light touch on the arm, a playful tease, a knowing smile—these go a long way.

Scenario: You're sitting next to your crush at a movie night. During a funny scene, you lightly touch their arm and share a laugh. It's subtle but effective.

Compliments

We've mentioned this, but it's worth repeating. Compliments should be sincere and specific.

Scenario: You're talking to your crush, and you notice they've done something different with their look. You say, "I really like how you did your makeup today. It's subtle but really highlights your eyes." Specific and sincere.

Mirroring

Subtly mimic their body language. It creates a sense of connection and shows you're in sync.

Scenario: During a conversation, you notice your crush leans in when they talk. You subtly do the same. This mirroring makes them feel more connected to you without them even realizing why.

Handling Rejection

Not everyone will respond to your Rizz, and that's okay. Handling rejection with grace is a sign of true Rizz mastery.

Don't Take It Personally

Rejection isn't a reflection of your worth. Sometimes, it's just not the right time or person.

Scenario: You muster up the courage to ask your crush out, but they turn you down. Instead of sulking, you smile and say, "No worries, maybe another time." Your cool response leaves a positive impression.

Learn and Move On

Use rejection as a learning experience. What can you improve for next time?

Scenario: After getting turned down, you reflect on the situation. Maybe your approach was too direct, or the timing was off. You adjust your strategy for the future.

Social Skills Boost

Improving your social skills can significantly enhance your Rizz. Here are some exercises to help you out:

Join Clubs or Groups

Being part of a club or group helps you meet new people and practice your social skills.

Scenario: You join the school's drama club. You get to interact with different people, and performing helps build your confidence. Plus, you never know, your crush might be into theater too!

Host Gatherings

Organize small get-togethers with friends. It's a great way to practice being a host and making people feel comfortable.

Scenario: You invite a few friends over for a movie night. You make sure everyone's having a good time, starting conversations, and ensuring everyone's included. Your efforts don't go unnoticed.

Attend Social Events

Go to parties, school dances, and other social events. The more you expose yourself to social settings, the better you'll get.

Scenario: You decide to attend a school dance. Even if you're nervous at first, you push yourself to talk to new people. By the end of the night, you've made new friends and boosted your confidence.

Chapter 4: Rizz King/Queen: Achieve Your Goal

You Made It!

Congratulations! You've made it to the top of the Rizz pyramid. You're officially a Rizz King or Queen. But with great power comes great responsibility. Stay humble, stay cool, and keep spreading those good vibes.

Positive Affirmations

You're a total boss. Remember that. Wake up every day and tell yourself:

- "I am awesome."
- "I've got the best Rizz in town."
- "I can charm anyone, anytime, anywhere."

Repeating positive affirmations helps reinforce your confidence and keep your Rizz game strong.

Keep Improving

Even Rizz royalty can always get better. Keep working on your social skills, stay updated with the latest trends, and never stop learning. The world of Rizz is ever-evolving, and so should you.

Stay Informed

Keep up with current events, popular culture, and trends. Being knowledgeable makes you more interesting and engaging in conversations.

Scenario: You read up on the latest trends in fashion and pop culture. When your crush mentions a trending topic, you can contribute to the conversation with confidence, showing that you're in the know.

Self-Reflection

Regularly reflect on your interactions. What went well? What could have been better?

The audience is captivated, and you receive a round of applause. Overcoming your fear not only boosts your confidence but also elevates your Rizz.

. Chapter 3: You're Getting There: Tips and Tricks

Smooth Moves

You're starting to get the hang of this Rizz thing, but let's take it up a notch with some next-level tips and tricks.

Compliments: The Right Way

Give genuine compliments. Notice something unique about the person and mention it. But don't overdo it; nobody likes a kiss-up. A well-placed compliment can make someone's day and make you stand out.

Scenario 1: Complimenting a Classmate

You're sitting next to your crush in class. You notice they've got a cool new haircut. Instead of just thinking it, you say, "Hey, I really like your haircut. It suits you." A simple compliment can make their day and make you stand out.

Scenario 2: Complimenting a Friend

Your friend has been working hard on a project and finally finishes it. You genuinely compliment their effort and creativity, "You did an amazing job on that project. It really shows how talented you are." Your friend feels appreciated, and your bond strengthens.

Humor: The Universal Lubricant

A good sense of humor is a one-way ticket to Rizz-ville. Crack jokes, be witty, and don't take yourself too seriously. Laughter is the best glue in any social situation.

Scenario 3: Lightening Up the Mood

You're at lunch with your friends, and the conversation is dragging. You crack a joke about the cafeteria food, and everyone bursts into laughter. Your ability to lighten the mood makes you the center of attention.

Scenario 4: Handling an Awkward Moment

You're on a date, and there's a sudden awkward silence. Instead of panicking, you make a light-hearted comment about the situation, "Wow, I never knew silence could be this loud!" Your date laughs, and the awkwardness dissipates.

Mystery: Keep Them Guessing

Keep a little mystery about you. Don't spill all your beans in the first conversation. Leave them wanting more. Be intriguing, like a Netflix show with endless cliffhangers.

Scenario 5: The Intriguing Hobby

You're on a first date, and instead of sharing your entire life story, you give just enough information to keep your date interested. You mention a cool hobby but don't go into details. They'll be curious and want to know more.

Scenario 6: Social Media Tease

You post a picture of a beautiful location on your social media with a vague caption. Your friends and followers are intrigued and start asking questions. This mystery keeps people engaged and curious about your adventures.

Social Media Rizz

Your online presence is just as important as IRL. Your Instagram, TikTok, and whatever other platforms you're on should scream Rizz.

Quality over Quantity

Post your best photos, the ones where you look like a snack. It's better to post one great photo a week than seven mediocre ones. Quality always wins.

Scenario 7: The Perfect Profile Pic

You're out with friends, and you take a killer group photo. Instead of posting every picture from the night, you pick the best one where you look confident and happy. Your followers will notice the quality over the quantity.

Engage

Comment on posts, reply to stories, and slide into DMs like a pro. Just don't be creepy. Engagement shows you're interested and active.

Scenario 8: Sliding into DMs

Your crush posts a picture of their new puppy. You leave a funny comment like, "I think your puppy just stole my heart!" It's light, engaging, and gets you noticed.

Memes: Share the Laughter

Share funny memes. Everyone loves a good meme. It shows you have a sense of humor and keeps the vibe light.

Scenario 9: Meme Master

You find a hilarious meme about school and share it on your story. Your crush replies with a laughing emoji, and just like that, you've started a conversation.

The Art of Flirting

Flirting is an essential Rizz skill. Here's how to do it without coming off as a total weirdo.

Subtlety: Less is More

A light touch on the arm, a playful tease, a knowing smile—these go a long way. Flirting should be fun and light-hearted, not intense and creepy.

Scenario 10: Movie Night Flirt

You're sitting next to your crush at a movie night. During a funny scene, you lightly touch their arm and share a laugh. It's subtle but effective.

Compliments: Sincere and Specific

We've mentioned this, but it's worth repeating. Compliments should be sincere and specific. This shows you're paying attention and genuinely appreciate them.

Scenario 11: The Thoughtful Compliment

You're talking to your crush, and you notice they've done something different with their look. You say, "I really like how you did your makeup today. It's subtle but really highlights your eyes." Specific and sincere.

Mirroring: The Subtle Sync

Subtly mimic their body language. It creates a sense of connection and shows you're in sync. This can be as simple as matching their posture or using similar gestures.

Scenario 12: Conversation Mirroring

During a conversation, you notice your crush leans in when they talk. You subtly do the same. This mirroring makes them feel more connected to you without them even realizing why.

Storytelling: Captivate with Tales

Good Rizz includes being a great storyteller. Share interesting, funny, or exciting stories about your experiences. This not only entertains but also gives people a glimpse into your life.

Scenario 13: The Epic Tale

You're hanging out with friends, and someone mentions traveling. You share a funny story about getting lost in a new city and the hilarious adventures that followed. Everyone is captivated by your story and your ability to make even a mishap sound exciting.

Listening: Show You Care

Great Rizz isn't just about talking; it's about listening too. Pay attention to what others are saying, ask follow-up questions, and show genuine interest. This makes people feel valued and important.

Scenario 14: The Attentive Listener

Your friend is talking about a problem they're facing. Instead of just nodding, you actively listen, ask thoughtful questions, and offer your support. Your friend appreciates your attention and feels closer to you.

Humor: Playful Teasing

A little playful teasing can show confidence and interest. Just make sure it's light-hearted and never mean-spirited.

Scenario 15: Playful Tease

You're talking to your crush about their favorite sports team. You playfully tease them about a recent loss, but in a fun and light-hearted way. They laugh, and it creates a playful dynamic between you.

Knowing When to Walk Away

Part of having Rizz is knowing when to walk away. If someone isn't reciprocating your interest or you're feeling uncomfortable, it's okay to step back. Confidence means not forcing anything and respecting both your own boundaries and others'.

Scenario 16: The Respectful Exit

You're at a party, and the person you're talking to seems uninterested. Instead of forcing the conversation, you politely excuse yourself and join another group. This shows you're confident enough to walk away and not desperate for attention.

Compliment Sandwich

A compliment sandwich is when you give a compliment, offer constructive feedback, and then end with another compliment. This technique is great for keeping the vibe positive.

Scenario 17: The Perfect Balance

Your friend asks for your opinion on their new outfit.
You say, "I love the color of your shirt; it really brings
out your eyes. Maybe try a different pair of shoes to
match, but overall, you look fantastic." This approach
shows you care and want to help without being harsh

Chapter 4: Rizz King/Queen: Achieve Your Goal

You Made It!

Congratulations! You've made it to the top of the Rizz pyramid. You're officially a Rizz King or Queen. But with great power comes great responsibility. Stay humble, stay cool, and keep spreading those good vibes.

Positive Affirmations

You're a total boss. Remember that. Wake up every day and tell yourself:

- "I am awesome."
- "I've got the best Rizz in town."
- "I can charm anyone, anytime, anywhere."

These affirmations aren't just words; they're a mindset. Start your day with positivity, and your Rizz will naturally shine through.

Keep Improving

Even Rizz royalty can always get better. Keep working on your social skills, stay updated with the latest trends, and never stop learning. The world of Rizz is ever-evolving, and so should you.

Scenario 1: Continuous Learning

You're already great at conversations, but you decide to take it further by reading about body language. This extra knowledge helps you read people better and enhances your social interactions. Always be a student of life and keep sharpening your Rizz.

Give Back

Now that you're at the top, it's time to help others. Be a mentor to your less Rizzed-up friends. Share your wisdom and watch them blossom into Rizz stars. Remember, the more you give, the more you get.

Scenario 2: Mentoring a Friend

You notice a friend struggling to talk to their crush. You give them a few tips from this book, and next thing you know, they're having a great conversation. Seeing them succeed feels just as good as your own success.

Stay Authentic

Lastly, never lose sight of who you are.

Made in the USA
Las Vegas, NV
11 December 2024